Iran on the Verge of a Revolution

We Can and We Must

Excerpts of Maryam Rajavi's Messages and Speeches

May to July 2022

Iran on the Verge of Revolution
We Can and We Must
Excerpts of Maryam Rajavi's Messages and Speeches
May to July 2022

ISBN:
978-2-491615-09-3
Published December 2022 by
National Council of Resistance of Iran
15 rue des Gords, 95430 Auvers sur Oise- France

Table of Contents

Resistance's Summit 2022...5

International dignitaries, lawmakers attend Resistance's summit 21

Maryam Rajavi's message to demonstration for a Free Iran in Berlin 33

Commemoration of the great Mossadeq.........................45

NCRI session on the Council's 41st Founding Anniversary..53

Global campaign against the disgraceful treaty between Belgium and the Iranian regime 71

Maryam Rajavi's message to the demonstration of freedom-loving Iranians in Stockholm 81

US Secretary of State Mike Pompeo's visit to Ashraf-3 ...91

Mike Pence's visit to Ashraf 3 103

Professor Richard Roberts, winner of the 1993 Nobel Prize visits Ashraf 3 117

Resistance's Summit 2022

"We Can and We Must"

The Free Iran World Summit - 2022 saw the participation of Iranians and political dignitaries from 101 countries around the world.

At this gathering, where Maryam Rajavi was also present and gave a speech, numerous political officials were in attendance and many of them spoke. They included two former presidents, 9 prime ministers, 3 parliament speakers, national security advisors, 29 former ministers from different countries, 79 lawmakers from Canada and European and Arab countries, and dozens of former US officials and political figures from around the globe. In addition, 42 senators and representatives from the US Congress sent video messages in support of the event.

At the beginning of this gathering, Mrs. Maryam Rajavi, the President-elect of the National Council of Resistance of Iran, provided an in-depth analysis of the clerical regime's circumstances and the revolutionary state of Iranian society.

Iran on the brink of change and of the clerical regime's overthrow

Greetings to my fellow compatriots across Iran,
To the Resistance Units, and to you, supporters of the Iranian Resistance around the world.

The free Iran you have come to welcome is surging amid the blazing flames of uprisings, successive failures of religious fascism, and in step with the advances of the democratic alternative to the clerical regime.

In the past year, the Iranian people's struggle has stood out because of the continued uprisings and protests nationwide, the Resistance Units' brilliant operations and campaigns against repression, and the Iranian Resistance's advancements on the social, political, legal, and international scenes.

Raisi's appointment backfired

But today, I would like to take a broader look at the enemies of the Iranian people, whose pathetic predicament represents a clear indication of the final phase of the mullahs' regime.

Ebrahim Raisi's appointment as president and a candidate to succeed Ali Khamenei, which the supreme leader described as the first and most important development in last year's sham election, backfired.

In addition to suppression that is always critical and decisive for the mullahs' survival, Hassan Rouhani saw the solution to problems and crises, including water shortages, in the JCPOA. In this way, he was asking Khamenei to grant him a larger share of power.

However, Khamenei, for whom the most important red line is preserving the regime and his own hegemony, knows to where the slightest schism in this respect leads. Therefore, he saw the solution in making the regime more monolithic. Playing cat and mouse in the nuclear talks, he is dragging out the negotiations to acquire the atomic bomb, as the guarantee for the religious dictatorship's survival.

For two years, Khamenei talked about "a young Hezbollahi government," which he considered the solution to the regime's internal and external crises. But Khamenei's desired government was dead on arrival. It not only failed to be the solution, but ex-acerbated the problems, seriously aggravating the regime's problems and crises. It in fact inspired the uprisings, with the chant of "Death to Raisi" becoming the rallying cry of the protest movement.

The murderer of the People's Mojahedin (PMOI/MEK) had come to block their path, but was checkmated by the ascension of the campaign undertaken by this movement and the Resistance Units in the framework of the Iranian people's uprisings.

In a word, Raisi's selection, perceived to act as the regime's savior, emerged as a signal to its end. As Massoud Rajavi, the Leader of the Iranian Resistance, stated, Rai-si's appointment was "the most obvious indicator of the phase of the (regime's) over-throw."

Is Iran on the brink of a revolution and of the regime's overthrow?

When addressing the issue of Iran, the main and most logical question, which encompasses all other questions is whether Iran is really on the brink of a revolution and whether the regime is on the verge of being overthrown? Are we really correct about this or are we exaggerating?

The mullahs say this is an exaggeration that makes the circumstances seem worse than they are. But, if we take a look at the people, their protests and their slogans, the claims by Khamenei and Raisi prove invalid.

> *The Iranian people's explosive power is far greater than any nuclear bomb. But even if the regime were to retreat from acquiring the atomic bomb, it would be drinking a poison chalice that would expedite the process of being overthrown.*

A glance at Iranian cities, and the unrelenting uprisings by millions of retirees, teachers, workers, nurses, and people fed up with high prices and inflation, makes it palpably clear that no exaggeration is at play. Ironically, the state of the regime is worse than what the press and the media report.

Over the past year, in addition to nationwide uprisings, Iranian teachers held 17 nationwide protests. Retirees took to the streets across the country 15 times.

Teachers cry, "The teachers' movement is ready for an uprising."

The arisen retirees say, "How much longer do we have to endure humiliation? Either death or life."

Isfahan's farmers chant, "Armies (of people) have come to wage war on the leader (Khamenei)."

The bereaved and rebellious people of Abadan roar, "Death to Raisi."

Protesters in Tehran shout, "Guns, tanks, are no longer effective, Khamenei must be killed."

Yes, this cry is Iran's cry. As Massoud Rajavi said, "Iran and her enchained people have risen up, and dawn is near."

Now, even the Revolutionary Guards Corps (IRGC), the central pillar of the religious dictatorship, is facing incredible changes, trepidation, and tremors.

This marks the failure of Khamenei's strategy of contraction, in that instead of unity and cohesion, it has afflicted the regime with more contradictions, schism, and conflcts. In a religious dictatorship that is rotten to core, Khamenei has now lost trust in the IRGC's top brass and even in the division in charge of his own protection.

We ask the world community to recognize the struggle of the rebellious youths against the terrorist IRGC to overthrow the ruling religious tyranny

Khamenei's acting representative in the IRGC said, "We will not allow viruses and termites to enter the totality of the IRGC." The IRGC's general commander has also declared, "The enemy wants to render us hollow from within, and this is the most dangerous form of attack."

We tell them: no, you are mistaken. What the Iranian people and Resistance are after is the complete destruction of the IRGC as the only way bringing about the overthrow of the religious dictatorship.

The pathetic and feeble state of the IRGC is like a bloodthirsty octopus sinking in the quagmire of 40 years of crimes but continuing to use all the means at its disposal to block freedom for the Iranian people.

What is the solution? There is one and only one solution: the definitive destruction and dismantling of the Revolutionary Guards by the uprisings and the Iranian people's great army of freedom; by the rebellious cities and Resistance Units, by the widespread support of various strata of people who have risen up and whose pro-tests are depriving the regime of a respite.

Iran and the rise of Resistance Units

From June 20, 2021, to June 20, 2022, the Resistance Units have carried out more than 2,350 campaigns against repression throughout Iran to pave the way for uprisings, 85% of which have been successful. The names and particulars of those arrested have been submitted to the international bodies by their friends and family members.

Reportedly, the IRGC is drawing up the maps of each and every city in an attempt to identify the areas prone to uprisings and districts whose population support the MEK. We tell them not to bother. The centers where uprisings erupt and locations where the Resistance Units relentlessly emerge are all the alleys and streets in every city across the country.

A month ago, Khamenei tried to console the Judiciary's executioners by saying that just as the regime survived the face-off with the Mojahedin in 1981, it will also put this year behind. In his words, "The God of 2022 is the same God as the God of 1981."

Yes, your idol, namely, the idol of flogging, executions, plunder, and massacre, is of course the same as it was back in 1981. However, since that year until now, our people and Resistance have become a thousand times more determined and battle-hardened. And the God of the heroic people of Iran is resolved to annihilate you.

To you, the enemies of the people of Iran, I say: It's great that you have not forgotten the internal war and the face-off with the PMOI/MEK in 1981. But it would serve you better if you always remember the Eternal Light operation and the National Liberation

In a word, Raisi's selection, perceived to act as the regime's savior, emerged as a sig-nal to its end. As Massoud Rajavi, the Leader of the Iranian Resistance, stated, Rai-si's appointment was "the most obvious indicator of the phase of the (regime's) over-throw."

What is the solution? There is one and only one solution: the definitive destruction and dismantling of the Revolutionary Guards by the uprisings and the Iranian people's great army of freedom, by the rebellious cities and Resistance Units, by the widespread support of various strata of people who have risen up and whose protests are depriving the regime of a respite

Army advancing to the gates of Kermanshah, in western Iran. Also, never forget the Ashura anniversary in December 2009, when the rebellious and Mojahed protesters advanced to the vicinity of Khamenei's headquarters. And you should never forget the nightmare of the November 2019 uprising.

By the way, you can thank your idol every day for having escaped being overthrown. But our people need to succeed only once at which point no trace of religious tyranny will be left.

The regime's nuclear impasse

The gambit of appointing henchman Raisi, which Khamenei believed was a cure-all, has failed. On the other hand, the strategy of Resistance Units and 1,000 bastions of Resistance was confirmed.

The Intelligence Ministry failed in its conspiracy to derail and distort the identity of the Call for Justice Movement when a criminal perpetrator of the 1988 massacre was arrested in Sweden. The scheme, similar to the hijacking of the 1979 anti-monarchical Revolution backfired. The world saw that one of the murderers of the PMOI and other political prisoners received maximum punishment.

As for the nuclear issue, Khamenei cannot pull himself out of the vicious cycle of the JCPOA. He is at a complete impasse, and whichever way he turns, he would be the first loser. And if he continues the policy of the last 18 months, he is going down the slippery slope of being overthrown.

Now, with Raisi, the regime has entered a phase where even a nuclear bomb cannot save it.

The Iranian people's explosive power is far greater than any nuclear bomb. But even if the regime were to retreat from acquiring the atomic bomb, it would be drinking a poison chalice that would expedite the process of being overthrown.

We tell the mullahs: Choose whichever path you desire and do so quicker. In any case, uprisings and overthrow are awaiting.

We only recommend that you keep an eye on your negotiating team. Surround them with some of Khamenei's representatives and IRGC counter-intelligence agents so that you would not have to arrest and imprison them for espionage like the previous teams.

What the past and present actors say

If Iran is really on the verge of a revolution and the clerical regime's overthrow? Let's see what the past and present actors are saying. And more significantly, how will the future unfold? The mullahs say one cannot and must not overthrow the regime. The Shah says you were wrong to overthrow me. Don't look for democracy and human rights except in rhetoric!

Yes, their objective is to pacify and derail the uprisings by sowing discord.

Therefore, to determine the nature of every person or group, one must ask them:

-Yes or no to the overthrow of the velayat-e faqih in its entirety?

-Which one do they agree with? The dismantling of the IRGC or collaborating with it?

-Whether they condemn the crimes, executions, and repression under the monarchical dictatorship and distance themselves from them?

Furthermore, any claimants of hereditary or non-hereditary alternatives must be asked what they have done so far. What is their political background and history of struggle? What price have they paid? What have they sacrificed for freedom and what price have they paid or are paying for it?

One says he is proud to have defected from the regime's ranks. Another boasts that he was once a so-called reformer or was expelled from one of the regime's factions. And a third claims that the blood of his despotic and criminal father and grandfather runs in his veins. Their motto is to return to the monarchical dictatorship. At the same time, they can be traced back to Khamenei's circle or to the IRGC.

Yes, they promote helplessness and hopelessness. The Shah and the mullahs over-look the outcome of 100 years of suffering and sacrifice embodied in the PMOI/MEK and the democratic alternative, the National Council of Resistance of Iran, to justify the continuation of the religious dictatorship.

Standing face-to-face with them is a generation with a historical and social mission. A generation that has paid the price of remaining steadfast in its ideals with a galaxy of martyrs since June 20, 1981. The massacre of its prisoners in 1988 is only one example.

In the fight against religious fascism, this generation, enduring several bloodbaths, has gone through difficult and complex trials and tribulations. Yes, this generation has learned from Massoud [Rajavi] to overcome deadlocks with ever-greater sacrifice, and to make the impossible, possible with a greater determination and to win victory.

The experience of resistance in Ukraine

Now, the example of Ukraine is before us. Five months of fire and blood have passed. Everyone sees the post-World War II's 77-year history has turned a page. The Ukrainian people, representatives, and leadership have become examples to follow in Europe by reviving the tradition of sacrifice and paying the price of resistance.

The human and utopian values that had gathered dust are being revived one after the other.

Today, the rebels in Ukraine are building tomorrow's history. Nobody will forget this. They took up arms, fought, and immortalized their resistance, regardless of the short-term results. We stand up and applaud them and the Ukrainian delegation here.

We can and we must

Now, let us imagine for a moment what would have happened to them and Europe if there had been no resistance in Ukraine and if they had not stood up to fight? What would have been their fate and, indeed, the fate of Europe?

This is the very question that our Resistance has been facing for 40 years. The secret to our Resistance, too, is offering love and the willingness to pay. Love for the people's freedom and liberation is the infinite source of human strength. This is where faith in victory emanates from. This is where the power to attack repression and suppression starts running in everyone's veins.

It inspires millions and millions of oppressed, battered, and plundered people to demand justice. It weakens and undermines the decadent and weary mullahs and their flagging regiment of revolutionary guards and criminals.

Yes, with such faith, you, the PMOI/MEK, the activists, the Resistance Units, and supporters of the Iranian Resistance can break down the religious fascism's machinery of murder and repression. We can and must hoist the lag of freedom and the people's sovereignty and a republic in our homeland.

Indeed, is "we can, and we must" just a slogan and a claim, or will it become reality? Is it reserved only for the elite, or does it belong to whoever chooses it? From here, I ask you, wherever you are and in the oppressed Iran, who can hear me: Are you among those who choose this path and this tradition of emancipation?

Yes, we can and must sing about Iran's freedom,
With an ideal that never sets,
We can forever destroy the castle of those spreading darkness
We can and must sing about Iran's freedom
Yes, we have come to help hope and convictions flourish, so that the wall of repression is broken, and the path to overthrowing the religious tyranny is opened, so that freedom, democracy, equality and a republic are established in Iran.
Whatever the cost, we will triumph in our great mission to transfer sovereignty to the Iranian people and their republic.
Yes, the dawn is near.
You, who have been enchained all this time,
You only have to take one more leap to break the trap
One step remains, one leap, and one stride.

> *Yes, we have come to help hope and convictions flourish, so that the wall of repression is broken, and the path to overthrowing the religious tyranny is opened, so that freedom, democracy, equality and a republic are established in Iran.*
> *Whatever the cost, we will triumph in our great mission to transfer sovereignty to the Iranian people and their republic*

We call upon all our compatriots, especially the courageous youth, to support the Resistance Units, the rebellious cities, and the arisen people.

We ask the world community to recognize the struggle of the rebellious youths against the terrorist IRGC to overthrow the ruling religious tyranny.

May you be victorious

International dignitaries, lawmakers attend Resistance's summit

On the second day of the Free Iran World Summit, a group of legislators and political and international personalities from different countries around the world, including delegations of parliamentarians from European countries, the Arab World, and American dignitaries, participated and gave speeches. At the beginning of this meeting, Maryam Rajavi explained the situation of the clerical regime and the missing link in Western governments' policies.

The only right and effective response to religious fascism is firmness not caving in

I am truly delighted to see you again. Over the past two years, we were unfortunately deprived of getting together. Ashraf residents are thrilled to see you here in Ashraf-3 because they can see their friends on difficult days. Those were challenging days, but we overcame all the obstacles with your help and support.

Indeed, you have visited the Iranian Resistance's museum, which offers only a glimpse of the Iranian people's pain and suffering and the Mojahedin's glorious resistance against the regime.

Three realities about Iran

I want to use this opportunity to review the circumstances in Iran.

Three truths about Iran provide a clear picture to every audience. First, the regime is rotten to the core. Second, the protest movement continues in Iran. And third is the role of the Iranian Resistance in leading the situation towards the regime's overthrow.

The mullahs are trying to hide, through adventure, threats, and hype, their fear of the regime's only rival, the Iranian people's Resistance, which is their Achilles heel.

You, dear friends, have targeted precisely this fundamental weakness of the regime by standing by the Iranian people's struggle for freedom and democracy. The solidarity of various tendencies in the Arab and Western worlds with the Iranian people's struggle is not acceptable to the mullahs.

Just recently, 5,000 members of the Resistance Units in Iran sent video messages declaring their readiness to overthrow the regime. The common phrase in their statements was "we can and we must." We can, and we must, overthrow the religious fascism in Iran. And the Iranian people and Resistance are capable of doing so.

This is a major stride in the Iranian Resistance's strategy that is working to organize the rebellious youths in Iran so that in combination with the popular uprisings, they can remove the regime from the Iranian people's path to freedom.

The determining factors in the Iranian situation are changing. One is the Iranian society, which is moving towards overthrowing the regime. The other is the regime's dire circumstances. Today, one of Khamenei's urgent problems is the frequent defections from the Revolutionary Guards Corps (IRGC).

A revealing development in recent weeks was the dismissal of a number of the highest IRGC commanders. They included the commander of the special division in charge of Khamenei's protection and the commander of the IRGC's Intelligence Organization.

Is the Iranian regime weak or strong?

Those unaware of the situation in Iran and the actual state of the mullahs think that the regime's export of terrorism or the use of drones and missiles against neighboring countries is a sign of power. Of course, this is a profound mistake.

Domestic suppression or missile launches and war mongering abroad are critical to the survival of the religious fascism. Therefore, the day they give those up, the regime will cease to exist. A dying viper stings until the last moment.

The only way to push back the regime is firmness, and of course, the determining element is the Iranian Resistance.

Our friends from Arab and Muslim countries can recall that Khomeini, the regime's founder, was at war with the neighboring country, Iraq, for eight years.

Khomeini used to say he would continue the war until the

> *The whole issue is that assistance to the mullahs to prevent their downfall must be stopped. A policy that has for the past three decades prevented democratic change in Iran must be put aside.*

destruction of the last brick of the buildings in Tehran. While in the summer of 1982, it was possible to end the war and establish peace, Khomeini and his regime prevented it. Eventually, the successful operations of the National Liberation Army and Khomeini's fear of being overthrown forced him to accept the ceasefire. Even then, he acknowledged, I am drinking the poison chalice of the ceasefire.

Currently, the weakness of the regime can be seen in several significant developments, including the continuation of the protest movement, the expansion of the Resistance's network and its operations inside Iran, the mullahs' incapability to resolve the social and economic problems, the defections from the IRGC, and the regime's failure to continue its theatrics about reform and moderation.

Appeasing the savage mullahs

For this reason, the clerical regime has never been so much in need of the West's appeasement. The mullahs show claws and teeth and churn out anti-Western rhetoric because they need to benefit from the West's security, political, and financial concessions.

Unfortunately, Western governments have not learned from the disasters of appeasing the mullahs' regime in the past three decades. The recent treaty between Belgium and the mullahs to hand over a bomb-carrying diplomat-terrorist despite his conviction by the Belgian Judiciary is an example of this policy. Iranians and supporters of the Iranian Resistance protested this disgraceful deal by holding demonstrations, rallies, and sit-ins in various countries.

Such perseverance, coupled with the Iranian Resistance's legal actions, has stopped the terrorist's transfer to Iran. The Court of Appeals of Belgium has undertaken to examine the case.

In the past four decades, there has never been an example where swapping the regime's imprisoned terrorists for western hostages did not subsequently endanger the lives of western citizens.

Another example is the regime's nuclear program.

The history of the mullahs' step-by-step approach to the atomic bomb is the same as the history of giving incentives to the regime.

While Western governments have sat idle for the last two years, the regime has used the opportunity to acquire the bomb, whereas a decisive policy could have stopped them.

One more example is Western governments' turning a blind eye on human rights violations in Iran.

During the uprising in November 2019, the IRGC received direct orders from Khamenei and massacred at least 1,500 young men and women. Unfortunately, the West chose to remain silent; the same catastrophic silence the West adopted towards the massacre of 30,000 political prisoners in 1988.

In a series of major revelations three months ago, the Iranian Resistance exposed millions of documents from the clerical regime's Prisons Organization.

I want to recall just one paragraph from those documents: 5,370 prisoners are condemned to death or retribution. Fifty-one of them are sentenced to stoning. Sixty minors are among these death-row prisoners.

Is it truly worthy of humanity to turn a blind eye on these savageries?

The mullahs are so confident of the West's conciliation that they have sent many of their Intelligence Ministry and Quds

Force agents to live in Europe and the U.S. as sleeper cells. There is no shortage of intelligence reports indicating that the mullahs procure from European markets both the equipment needed for their nuclear program and the means of suppressing the Iranian people.

The crux of the matter is why when the Iranian society is preparing to overthrow the regime, European governments side with the mullahs?

The whole issue is that such assistance to the mullahs to prevent their downfall must be stopped. A policy that has for the past three decades prevented democratic change in Iran must be put aside.

It is now more evident than ever that the Middle East, the Arab World, and the world of Islam, will not experience calm. They cannot remove the obstacles to their political and economic development unless the barriers are removed from the Iranian people's path to regime change.

The epicenter of the export of terrorism, fundamentalism, and belligerence in the Middle East, the clerical regime, must be eliminated.

The time has come for a new policy against the regime. The missing link in the policies of the European and American governments is their disregard for the Iranian people, especially their organized resistance. This approach has served the mullahs' regime.

The missing link of western politics

Yes, the time has come for a new policy against the regime. The missing link in the policies of the European and American governments is their disregard for the Iranian people, especially their organized resistance. This approach has served the mullahs' regime.

The governments of Europe and the United States should side with the Iranian people and their demands. Some specific actions are expected from the European governments and from the European Union.

1- Designating the entire Ministry of Intelligence and the IRGC as terrorist enti-ties;

2- Expelling intelligence and IRGC agents from European soil and depriving them of asylum and citizenship;

3- Referring the Iranian regime's dossier of terrorism, genocide, and crimes against humanity to the UN Security Council and the prosecution of Khame-nei, Raisi, and other regime leaders;

4- Predicating political and economic relations with the regime on stopping the execution and export of terrorism by the mullahs' regime; and

5- Recognizing the struggle of rebellious youths in Iran against the terrorist IRGC to overthrow religious tyranny.

Of course, as the Iranian Resistance Leader Massoud Rajavi has constantly reiterat-ed: Regime change and overthrowing the mullahs is our responsibility. Our people and the revolutionary pioneers have undertaken this task.

The Iranian Resistance and the democratic alternative of the National Council of Resistance of Iran believe in a democratic republic, gender equality, and the separation of religion and state. They will be the standard-bearers of just relations based on respect for independence, national sovereignty, and coexistence with their neighbors and the entire world.
I am convinced we will always have you by our side in this liberating struggle.
Thank you all.

> *The Iranian Resistance and the democratic alternative of the National Council of Resistance of Iran believe in a democratic republic, gender equality, and the separation of religion and state. They will be the standard-bearers of just relations based on respect for independence, national sovereignty, and coexistence with their neighbors and the entire world.*

Maryam Rajavi's message

to demonstration for

a Free Iran in Berlin

Free Iran demonstrations in Berlin

On Saturday, July 23, 2022, Free Iran demonstration was held at the Brandenburg Gate in Berlin. Thousands of freedom-loving Iranians and supporters of the main opposition Mujahedin-e Khalq (MEK) took part in the gathering. Mrs. Maryam Rajavi told the demonstration via a video message: Amidst the Iranian people's sea of suffering and blood, the tower of the regime's overthrow is rising, and the regime is trembling.

A number of German parliamentarians and personalities as well as representatives of Iranian communities in Germany spoke at the gathering in Berlin.

PIZZA e PASTA
PIZZA
We Support Maryam Rajavi's 10 Point Plan for a Free Iran

IRAN with MARYAM

نه به شاه
نه به شیخ
آری
به جمهوری
و دموکراسی

The correct response to religious fascism is "firmness," and not kowtowing

Rebellious friends of the Iranian Resistance,
Supporters of the uprisings,
Dear personalities and friends in Germany!

The arisen Iranians who are staging this huge and magnificent demonstration in Berlin, the Free Iran gathering in Germany.
Before all else, I want to ask what have you done to have prompted the mullahs are screaming against the Iranian Resistance?
What has happened can be summarized as such: Amid the Iranian people's pain and suffering, the overthrow of the regime has appeared on the horizon and the mullahs are trembling.

A pact with the devil

You are certainly aware of the latest developments. Following legal complaints by the NCRI and several international dignitaries, Brussel's Court of Appeals prohibited the government of Belgium from sending the Iranian regime's bomb-carrying diplomat-terrorist to Iran, predicating it on a substantive examination.
To do so was what we had wanted: to have time so that there would not be a surprise transfer of this diplomat-terrorist. The court is scheduled to address the merits of the request by the

Iran will be free and as Massoud Rajavi, the leader of the Iranian Resistance, said: No power in the world can prevent the Iranian people's uprising and freedom.

plaintiffs to prohibit Assadi's freedom.

The court's ruling came immediately after the adoption of a shameful treaty which Belgian parliamentarians said was a dark day. They said this was crazy and they cannot find proper words to describe it. They also said they were proud of many Iranians who had joined the campaign.

I have already said, and I reiterated that pinning hope on the release of an innocent Belgian hostage in Iran is one-step forward and 100 steps back because, in the future, no one will be safe. Every European and American citizen in Iran will become a potential hostage.

Is this not a pact with the devil against the security of European and American citizens, the Iranian people, and their Resistance? Indeed, what is the correct and effective policy against the religious fascism rul-ing Iran and its Gestapo?

The correct and effective response to religious fascism is one word, "firmness," and not kowtowing.

The mullahs' hostage-taking and blackmail

When the regime engages in extortion and blackmail. European governments should put the prosecution of the regime's president, Ebrahim Raisi, for crimes against humanity and genocide on the table. They should close the regime's embassies.

They should boycott and impose sanctions on the regime to force it to release the hostage.

In 2009, with their resistance and firmness, Ashraf residents forced Khamenei's puppet Prime Minister in Iraq to release our hostages and return them to Ashraf.

They and their friends are present at this gathering today. They went on a hunger strike for 72 days, including a seven-day dry hunger strike. At that time, Ashraf supporters were also on hunger strikes in most countries.

On the other hand, in pursuing the policy of blackmail, and engaging in a ridicu-lous theatric, the mullahs' Foreign Ministry has sanctioned 61 distinguished American personalities for supporting the PMOI/MEK, which is of course a badge of honor. Many of them were targets of the bombing plot against the Paris gathering in 2018.

The sanctioning of these personalities is added reason why the Belgian govern-ment must not release the bomb-carrying diplomat in violation of the UN Securi-ty Council's resolution 1373.

Eight prominent international jurists have stated that this treaty is "a failure of Europe's efforts to fight terrorism," and that mullahs must not be allowed to mock the enforcement of justice in Europe.

They invoked "national security" imperative, but with their own hands, they are making the security of the peoples of Europe vulnerable to state terrorism.

Nine prominent American figures wrote: This treaty allows the Iranian regime to establish its European terrorist command center in Belgium.

Gentlemen, do not allow this to happen. Let Brussels remain the seat of the Eu-ropean Union, not the headquarters of the mullahs' terrorism in Europe.

The mullahs have so far arrested at least 150 diplomats, journalists, business people, or Iranians with dual nationality in Iran. They have taken 104 western na-tionals hostage in Lebanon. But through your efforts, you made the world take a stand. You held protests in 18 countries and staged sit-ins in five countries including in Berlin.

You showed that there is an unrelenting Resistance, which is the voice, the repre-sentative, and the guardian of the rights of Iran and Iranians. Thus, we again tell European governments to not rear a snake in their sleeves.

The former German intelligence organization chief revealed the Iranian regime had been behind several terrorist operations after the signing of the JCPOA, but the Europeans kept silent because they did not want to jeopardize the Iran nucle-ar deal.

So, gentlemen, you missed out on the JCPOA and instead have to deal with the regime's terrorism while it is getting closer to a nuclear bomb. Truly, for how long do you want to let the monster of terrorism and fundamentalism take you for a ride?

What kind of a policy is this? Its victims are western nationals in Iran. Of course, the main victims have always been and continue to be the Iranian people and Re-sistance.

My Oath to the People of Iran

Here, I want my fellow compatriots to allow me say a few words for the first time about the conspiracies the regime has hatched and will continue to hatch against me. I want to say a few words from my heart about the regime's expressions of rage.

Since I joined the ranks of the resistance during the Shah's reign, I was prepared to sacrifice my life for freedom.

A few years later, when Khomeini shot by firing squads teenage boys and girls, some of whom worked with me, my heart went out to them, and I wished I could be in their place.

I have had this feeling hundreds of times, including when I was hearing my sisters were being executed or massacred in Gohardasht or Evin or other prisons all over Iran.

I have always envied and continue to envy them for their sacrifice, a common feeling among the Mojahedin when they lose the best and the brightest.

The mullahs have been planning to eliminate me for years. And every time in a different venue, in Paris, in Germany, in Villepinte, in Albania, and other an-nounced and unannounced cases.

Therefore, I say to the masterminds of these plans, Khamenei and his accomplic-es that from the mass killings of the 80s to the 1988 massacre to the massacres of Ashraf and Liberty, you have seen and experienced that killing and eliminating the PMOI/MEK is useless.

This generation has come to sacrifice everything for the freedom of its people. I am one of them, as well.

I wish by sacrificing my life, the killing of my compatriots in Iran could be stopped.

But the bloodthirsty tyrant is insatiable.

My oath to the Iranian people and my commitment to Massoud Rajavi - to my last breath and my last drop of blood - is to overthrow the mullahs' inhuman regime.

When the regime engages in extortion and blackmail. European governments should put the prosecution of the regime's president, Ebrahim Raisi, for crimes against humanity and genocide on the table. They should close the regime's embassies. They should boycott and impose sanctions on the regime to force it to release the hostage.

So, I tell the regime's supreme leader that if he thinks he can stop us by these conspiracies, he is gravely mistaken.

We will intensify the lames of the battle

And I must say the last word to our heroic people:
What should I pour at your feet to be worthy of you,
Because one couldn't say that my head and life is worthy enough.
Yesterday, I saw video and audio messages of more than 5,000 Resistance Units., who announced they are ready and said we can and we must over-throw this regime.
I hope this footage can be broadcast soon.
The situation has gotten to a point that neither the butcher Raisi nor a nuclear bomb are going to be effective.
The mullahs' ploys of trying to raise the dead and deposed shahs from the grave will not cure anything either.
The mullahs' regime is at the verge of the same grave in which the monarchy fell.
Yes, Iran will be free and as Massoud Rajavi, the leader of the Iranian Resistance, said: No power in the world can prevent the Iranian people's uprising and freedom.
May victory be yours.

*Commemoration of
the great Mossadeq*

To the great Mossadeq, we say, the Iranian nation is determined in its struggle for freedom

On the 70th anniversary of the Iranian people's great uprising on July 21, 1952, we salute Dr. Mohammad Mossadeq, the leader of the Iranian people's national movement against colonialism.

Mossadeq's noble message in the 17th court-martial session addressing the Shah and his mercenaries is a source of pride. His message rings out today more powerful and genuine than ever.

July 21, 1952, the test for the Iranian nation

As Dr. Mossadeq said on the first anniversary of that great uprising, "July 21 is unforgettable in the history of the Iranian people's ongoing struggles. Because on that day, all Iranians, of all classes and posts, acted in unison and did not rest until they achieved their objective."

We salute the martyrs of the national uprising of July 21, 1952, and join the great Mossadeq, in "offering our deep respect and honor" to the memory of those fallen in the path of freedom and liberty.

Indeed, paving the path to freedom and independence is only possible through the great sacrifice of the nation's best children and the suffering endured by the pioneers of this path.

This is why the Iranian nation's uprisings, from July 21, 1952, to June 20, 1981, are, as Dr. Mohammad Mosaddeq once said, "a crucible where the Iranian nation is refined, as gold is, from all its impurities of corruption and decay."

Today, 70 years after the July 21 uprising, on the 41st anniversary of the NCRI's founding, and as the Iranian people's resistance

> *Mossadeq was a statesman who nationalized Iran's oil industry, for which reason he is remembered as the pioneer of anti-colonialist movements in the Middle East and North Africa.*

has reached its highest peaks, I am proud to address the late leader, the great Mossadeq: As you dreamed, the Iranian nation is "determined to persevere and remain steadfast" in the struggle for freedom. "When the country's honor and independence are at stake, this nation prefers death to a life tainted with shame and disgrace."

The blood-drenched list of martyrs who laid down their lives in the struggle against the mullahs' dictatorship attests to such perseverance, from 30,000 victims of the 1988 massacre to the latest rebellious youths and members of the Resistance Units.

Mossadeq's uncompromising leadership

Mossadeq was a statesman who nationalized Iran's oil industry, for which reason he is remembered as the pioneer of anti-colonialist movements in the Middle East and North Africa.

Mossadeq's uncompromising leadership and his victory in defending the Iranian nation's rights at the UN Security Council and the International Court at the Hague, despite the efforts of the Shah and the colonialists, attest to the reality that it is possible to establish a democratic government in Iran that relies on people's votes, defends the nation's true interests, and is free of corruption and tyranny.

If on that day, the Shah's dictatorship had not prevented the continuity of Dr. Mossadeq's nationalist government;

if the shameful coup d'état of August 19, 1953, had not destroyed the yearning for freedom and nationalism;

if the Shah had not executed and imprisoned Mossadeq's supporters, especially Dr. Hossein Fatemi (his foreign minister), Iran would have no doubt been different today.

The Monarchic dictatorship followed up with arresting and executing the leaders of the People's Mojahedin and the Fedayeen, thus paving the way for Khomeini and his gang of criminals.

As Massoud Rajavi, the leader of the Iranian Resistance, said, "Mossadeq was not a person; he presented a roadmap. The attacks on him from all sides were aimed at his path and vision; the path to independence and freedom, and the path of not compromising with foreign colonialism, dictatorship, and reactionary currents inside Iran."

The Iranian people salute and honor the late leader of the Iranian national movement, who was not afraid of imprisonment, exile, and solitude in Ahmadabad, his hometown village.

He endured the demonization campaign by reactionaries and colonialists, as well as the campaigns of lies and accusations but persevered on ideal of the freedom and independence of Iran.

As he said, his only sin and that of the leaders of the Iranian people's struggle for freedom is that they have persevered in defense of liberty. They aspire for only one thing: "the Iranian people taking control of their destiny and no other factor than the people's will govern the country."

We honor Dr. Mossadeq's name and memory with his last

> **We say to the great Mossadeq: We said yes to the glorious mission and commitment placed on our shoulders in contemporary history. And we will raise aloft the Iranian people's flag of freedom and democratic republic on the peak of Damavand.**

message from his exile in Ahmadabad in December 1958. He told the "beloved and brave nation of Iran" to not fear any calamity in the noble path they started, and to continue their sacred movement.

Indeed, during the critical periods of struggle in these recent decades, Massoud Rajavi and the PMOI took Mossadeq's name and path to new heights, rendering it permanent in the history of the Iranian people's struggle.

We say to the great Mossadeq: We said yes to the glorious mission

> *If the shameful coup d'état of August 19, 1953, had not destroyed the yearning for freedom and nationalism; if the Shah had not executed and imprisoned Mossadeq's supporters, especially Dr. Hossein Fatemi (his foreign minister), Iran would have no doubt been different today.*

and commitment placed on our shoulders in contemporary history. And we will raise aloft the Iranian people's flag of freedom and democratic republic on the peak of Damavand. And on that day, your name, the great Mossadeq,

"Your great name will be engraved on all the leaves in this land, in stories, in whispers, and in songs, everywhere and every place forever."

Glory to Mossadeq!

Glory to the martyrs of July 21, 1952!

NCRI session
on the Council's 41st
Founding Anniversary

The National Council of Resistance of Iran (NCRI) held is midterm session on the 41st anniversary of its founding on July 28 and 29, 2022, chaired by Mrs. Maryam Rajavi, the NCRI's President-elect for the transitional period. Members and observers participated in the session from 10 countries, France, Germany, Sweden, the Netherlands, the United Kingdom, the United States, Italy, Switzerland, Belgium, and Albania.

In her remarks, Mrs. Rajavi underscored that the NCRI's 40th year was marked with the expansion of various aspects of its activities, including the upsurge in its efforts and the rise in the standing of the sole democratic alternative to the regime.

Discussions during the two-day session dealt with the Iranian regime's crisis-riddled state, the explosive situation of the society, the increase in the uprisings against high prices, protests by different sectors, the standing, and the achievements of the NCRI, international solidarity with the Iranian Resistance, and the worldwide campaigns against executions, other anti-human crimes and terrorism perpetrated by the clerical regime. Forty-five NCRI members and observers addressed the session which ended on midnight, July 29, 2022.

Maryam Rajavi's Speech at NCRI session on the Council's 41st Founding Anniversary

The alternative to the mullahs' regime has its roots in a long struggle against religious tyranny

Greetings to all friends and fellow members of the National Council of Resistance present here and in other countries.
And our warm greetings to all the dear sisters and brothers here and in other countries who have joined us as NCRI members or observers

To begin with, we honor the memory of Dr. Manouchehr Hezarkhani, the Chairman of the Culture and Arts Committee of the National Council of Resistance of Iran (NCRI). After 41 years, his seat in this assembly is empty, but his political and cultural legacy in the NCRI remains an inspiration to the generation that rose up to rebel and resist, overthrow the regime and win freedom.

Everyone remembers that wherever there was struggle and resistance, Dr. Hezarkhani was present and spoke about the legitimacy of the resistance with penetrating logic and eloquent language.

We remember that since 1981 and the founding of the NCRI, Dr. Hezarkhani's fraternal and friendly assistance in spirit, action, and with his pen to the NCRI Chairman was commendable and instructive.

We also honor the living memory of Dr. Samad Fathpour, a sincere friend of the Resistance, as well as our brother, the great Mojahed Abbas Modarresifar, with his long history of struggle in the Shah's prisons and then in Ashraf and Liberty camps [in Iraq]. We also honor the memory of my beloved sister, Hamideh Ta'ati, a member of the People's Mojahedin Organization of Iran (PMOI/MEK), who was a living example of struggle and courage.

Indeed, each of them were symbols of resistance and loyalty to the cause by dedicating their lives to the Iranian people's liberation.

We also honor the memory of the poet and activist author, Mr. Rahman Karimi, and Mr. Majid Taleghani who passed away due to illness.

Expansion of the battle fronts against the mullahs' regime

Since the previous summit, we have gone through a year marked by the expansion of the struggle fronts, the efforts of the Iranian Resistance and the democratic alternative, as well as the escalation of their activities.

This period coincided with the presidency of Ebrahim Raisi, the 1988 massacre henchman. This was a period when the mullahs' regime, entangled in internal and external crises, turned to its two usual tactics: executions and savage repression of women.

The number of executions recorded under Raisi amounted to at least 520 cases, which is far more than in previous years.

In five days alone, from July 23 to July 27, twenty prisoners, including two women, were executed.

Repression of women under the pretext of "mal-veiling,"

The repression of women in our country these days, under the pretext of "mal-veiling," which is invented by the mullahs, has taken unprecedented dimensions. Heartbreaking scenes of aggression against freedom-loving and honorable girls and women hurt the conscience of every human being.

The regime has expanded its suppression of women even to the cemeteries. They have been damaging the tombstones of women who display "improperly veiled" portraits.

Indeed, negotiating and talking with a regime that is a disgrace for contemporary humanity is shameful. It amounts to trampling on the values that the world has acquired at the cost of hundreds of millions of lives in recent centuries. The international community must reject the mullahs' regime.

Dear friends,

During this one-year period, the organized force of the resistance in the form of Resistance Units and Popular Resistance Councils has dramatically expanded.

The military assaults, targeting the bases of the Islamic Revolutionary Guard Corps (IRGC), about which you have certainly heard, have increased as well.

The latest case targeted the headquarters of the Special Units of the State Security Forces (SSF) that play a criminal role in the brutal suppression of the uprisings and the killing of young people.

Since January 27, 2022, the Resistance Units have seized the control of websites and servers of various regime agencies.

In October last year, the NCRI office in Washington, D.C. made an important disclosure about the regime's drone production and manufacturing centers.

Throughout the past year, at every opportunity, the People's Mojahedin Organization of Iran (PMOI/MEK) and the NCRI have advanced the movement of seeking justice for the victims of the 1988 massacre in legal, social and international arenas. This was done in the form of international conferences, publication of books, or conferences attended by world-renowned jurists.

There were also calls for an immediate investigation of the 1988 massacre, such as the appeal by 462 current and former UN officials, renowned lawyers, international court judges and authorities, and Nobel Prize laureates.

At the end of September last year, as a result of NCRI's legal

> *Since the previous summit, we have gone through a year marked by the expansion of the struggle fronts, the efforts of the Iranian Resistance and the democratic alternative, as well as the escalation of their activities.*

activities, the Swiss Federal Court issued a very important decision, which said that despite the passage of more than 30 years, the case regarding the assassination of Prof. Kazem Rajavi is not closed and should instead be investigated in the context of genocide and crimes against humanity. Both of these matters are not subject to any statute of limitations.

Throughout the year, in response to the events in Iran, the supporters of the Iranian Resistance organized many demonstrations and rallies in many major capitals of the world.

Confronting the mullahs' demonization and vilification campaigns against the PMOI and NCRI, the NCRI Counter-terrorism and Security Committee made public 26 confidential documents of the regime's Press TV. The documents show in part the behind-the-scenes production of documentaries, programs, and video clips against the PMOI for the mullahs' foreign ministry and judiciary, in exchange for large payments of money to the network of "friendly journalists."

The NCRI was able to play an important role in keeping Khamenei's IRGC on the U.S. list of terrorist groups.

On the other hand, the efforts of the PMOI and its supporters have helped expand global solidarity with the Iranian Resistance. The visits to Ashraf-3 by former U.S. Secretary of State Mike Pompeo, former U.S. Vice President Mike Pence, and former

European prime ministers and their explicit emphasis on the need to recognize the right of the Iranian people to resist and overthrow the regime is a new achievement for the Iranian people's Resistance movement.

In addition, there was a yearlong ceaseless campaign in Stockholm in conjunction with the trial of the regime's executioner Hamid Noury. The PMOI and the NCRI succeeded in foiling what was initially a complex conspiracy to discredit the Call for Justice Movement and to distort the identity of the PMOI victims of the 1988 massacre.

The unprecedented epic resistance of the political prisoners who remained faithful to their cause during the massacre was made clear for everyone inside Iran and around the world. It also underscored the need to bring the regime's Supreme Leader Ali Khamenei and its President Ebrahim Raisi to justice for committing crimes against humanity.

Finally, there was the campaign against the regime's treaty with Belgium to get back its jailed diplomat-terrorist, which was one of the most important chapters in last year's activities.

The first stage of this campaign lasted a total of 20 days. Our compatriots, supporters, and members of the Iranian Resistance in various countries protested and organized sit-ins and demonstrations. In the next stage, we started the political and legal campaigns, which are continuing.

The Brussels Court extended the ban on the extradition of the mullahs' bomb-carrying diplomat-terrorist until September 19 to deal with the content of the plaintiffs' request, which is an achievement for the Iranian Resistance's global campaign and the efforts of its supporters. For all that they have done, they are

to be congratulated.

In this campaign, what impressed everyone, including both the domestic and foreign media, as well as Belgian parliamentarians from the opposition parties and the ruling factions, and especially noteworthy for the regime itself, was the PMOI's and NCRI's mobilization and leadership capabilities.

Through the activities I briefly mentioned, the Iranian Resistance has been able to have a significant impact on intensifying the regime's crisis of overthrow over the past year.

In addition, the number of Iranians, especially young people, who join the Iranian Resistance increased and the quality of their influence was enhanced considerably.

The NCRI's platform for the establishment of a republic based on freedom and democracy, universal suffrage, the separation of religion and state, gender equality, and autonomy of ethnic groups has received more popular approval than ever before.

The NCRI has also achieved many successes in the daily struggle to expose the regime's vulnerability and deadlocks on the verge of overthrow. It has shown that the NCRI is the alternative and the solution, and promises a viable and concrete prospect.

The NCRI sets the yardstick in the fight for the regime's overthrow

When we talk about the alternative, it is not merely a hollow claim or a vague title that has no impact on the daily vicissitudes of the struggle against the regime.

Rather, we are referring to the guiding force and mechanism of advancement that determines the direction of the collection of all the activities in the struggle. It clarifies the steps to be taken, the direction, the slogan, the commonalities and contradictions, and it sets the priorities.

The alternative represents the solution to every problem faced by the movement in its daily struggle on a difficult and rough terrain. It shows the targets, distinguishes good from bad, differentiates right from wrong, and protects the assets of the Iranian people and Resistance from being stolen by the regime and its accomplices. In a word, the alternative is the yardstick in the struggle for the clerical regime's overthrow.

At this point, I would like to speak about the function of the NCRI, especially at a time when Iran is engulfed in a revolutionary state. The NCRI Chairman focused from the outset on Khamenei's roadmap and strategy of closing ranks in the regime, and said this represents the path toward the regime's overthrow. He stressed that it would be impossible for the regime to return to the previous balance of power. Moreover, he outlined a theory about the phenomenon of Raisi, which says that Raisi is "the outcome and clearest indicator of the phase of overthrow."

When it comes to the nuclear issue, he explained the theoretical and political perspective that with Raisi, we have entered a phase where even an atomic bomb will not be able to save the regime. He underlined the essential factor for the regime's repression, namely the IRGC, which he said is "the central organ of armed violence and repression and the main tool for preserving the religious dictatorship. It is not enough to blacklist it; it must be disbanded altogether."

With regard to social and economic issues, the NCRI has launched a persistent and non-stop campaign against Khamenei's sinister strategy during the Coronavirus pandemic. Even the state media wrote, "The opposition is doing its best (...) to put the government at the top of the list of culprits responsible for the increase in the death toll and cases of Coronavirus. Consequently, they unscrupulously introduce (Khamenei) as the one responsible for the death toll."

The NCRI has strongly reinforced the bonds between the oppressed ethnic minorities and the nationwide opposition through its actions and reactions. It has drawn public attention to the fact that this democratic alternative is the only source of support for the Baluch, Kurds and Arab compatriots nationwide. Countering the regime's decision to divide Sistan-and-Baluchestan into four provinces, the Resistance denounced the plan as a move to "sow discord in Sistan-and-Baluchestan," and called on the valiant Baluchies to rise up against it.

The NCRI strongly opposed the plan to divide the province of Khuzestan into two, and encouraged our compatriots in Khuzestan to protest against this plan, which only distracts attention from the uprising and sows divisions among the people of the province.

In the wake of the regime's bombing of some regions in the Iraqi Kurdistan, the NCRI chairman said, "To push back against the mullahs' regime in the bombing of innocent people and Iranian Kurdish parties in the border region, people must rise up in the oppressed cities of Iranian Kurdistan and throughout the country, as they did in the case of water shortages in Khuzestan."

During the uprising in Khuzestan, the NCRI Chairman emphasized the destructive role of the IRGC and said, "Khamenei's IRGC must stop deliberately drying up the marshes, which causes environmental disasters, especially for our Arab compatriots and get lost."

Furthermore, regarding the high prices, hunger and homelessness imposed on the people, the NCRI Chairman revealed the essence of Khamenei's policy.

Yes, the truth is that after the pandemic, Khamenei and Raisi want to massacre people through the imposition of high prices and hunger.

The National Council of Resistance says the following:

"We emphasize that Khamenei and his headquarters must completely abandon the one trillion dollars of assets amassed in the Executive Headquarters of Khomeini's Order (SETAD), the Mostazafan Foundation, the Astan-e-Quds Foundation, and the cooperatives of the IRGC, Bassij militia, and the State Security Forces. These funds should be used for the livelihood, employment, medical care, and education of the entire population."

The NCRI's platform for the establishment of a republic based on freedom and democracy, universal suffrage, the separation of religion and state, gender equality, and autonomy of ethnic groups has received more popular approval than ever before

Khamenei's attempt to divert the movement

As for the uprisings and the protest movement, the mullahs are trying to portray the protests as apolitical, with limited demands. They want to prevent them from joining with the main force of the uprising, namely the Resistance Units.

Khamenei has repeatedly tried to separate the "people's demands" from the "sabotage of a certain group." He wants to limit the Iranian people's roaring movement to the so-called civil rights struggle and complaints about marginal issues.

In contrast, the NCRI has in theory and practice, in their statements, positions, and efforts, guided the people's struggles to target Khamenei's headquarters, and have strengthened national solidarity against the ruling regime.

The NCRI also fought the regime's tactic of sending Bassij and Hezbollahi agents among protesters to spread deviatory slogans. The Iranian Resistance waged a political and theoretical campaign against all kinds of theatrics aimed at demoralizing the uprisings and stripping them of the spirit of overthrow.

The Iranian Resistance also refuted the claims of those who promote compromise with the regime, who propagate costless methods, which serve the survival of the religious tyranny. It also denounced the seasonal theatrics of spurious "alternatives."

Today, the protest movements in Iran are signified with the will to overthrow the clerical regime in Iran, a demand that is identified with the NCRI and the Iranian Resistance.

The slogans of "down with the dictator", "down with Raisi" and "down with Khamenei" have become common in the acts of protest.

We highlight the slogan "down with Khamenei - down with Raisi" as the Iranian people's main slogan and the general slogan of the uprisings to overthrow the regime.

The Iranian Resistance's other achievement was to forge bonds between the activities of Resistance Units and the oppressed people's reactions to the regime's repression and destruction of their homes.

Examples include the Resistance Units' activities in response to the inhumane destruction of the poor people's shelters by Khamenei's repressive agents in Zahedan, Khorramabad, Baharestan, and Robat-Karim.

Or the Resistance Units' response to the appalling insults and beatings of women under the pretext of being improperly veiled in Maragheh and other cities. Another example was seen in the attack on the regime court that sentenced Navid Afkari to death, or in protests against the execution of Iman Sabzikar, in Jonaqan. The Resistance Units have consistently targeted the mullahs' religious seminaries and centers, thereby highlighting two facts. One is the Iranian people's disgust with the mullahs' religious propaganda, and the other is the people's desire to separate religion from state, a desire that the NCRI has reflected in its plans since 40 years ago.

The process of quantitative and qualitative expansion of the

Resistance Units, including the audio and video messages sent by more than 5,000 members of these units, has once again demonstrated the broad-based support in society for the Iranian Resistance.

The fact is that a young and rebellious generation has turned to the anti-regime fighting force, to the democratic alternative, and to the struggle to overthrow the regime.

The number two man in the mullahs' Judiciary said, "For a period, it was thought that the PMOI/MEK was a small group without any supporters, so there is no need to talk about them. But we no longer think so and since 2021, heavy pressure was brought on countries that host the PMOI groups."

Yes, the Iranian Resistance has compelled the mullahs to regret their years of denying the PMOI's social base and to confess that they were wrong.

Finally, on the unity of popular forces against the religious dictatorship, the NCRI Chairman, drawing on the painful and bloody experience of the Iranian Resistance, defined this progressive and real solution in the following terms: "Unity and solidarity find their meaning and are tested in the field of action to overthrow the religious tyranny. This is the self-motivated and law-based mechanism that purifies the ranks of the movement

this alternative, with its set of programs, plans, views, and especially with its leadership in the battle against religious dictatorship, provides both the answer to the problems of today's struggle and the solution to the problems of tomorrow's Iran.

from residues of the Shah and the mullahs, from tyranny and dependence, and from opportunism."

The right response to the crisis in Iran

I would like to conclude by saying that the roots of this alternative have been strengthened in a long and bitter struggle against religious tyranny.

The force that opposes religious fascism has organized itself, developed plans and a program, and has paid the price for its day-to-day resistance.

And in recent years, as conditions have become more difficult, it has increased its capacity to shoulder heavier responsibilities and to fight on.

It has also maintained its political demarcations, democratic principles and values in defense of freedom, and protected them from the enemy.

If it were not for the will to oppose religious fascism at all costs in all cultural, social and political aspects, what would have happened to Iran and the Iranian people with the rule of this bloodthirsty and fearsome tyranny?

If we look at the turning points, from June 20, 1981, to July 25, 1988, the anniversary of the Iranian National Liberation Army's Operation Eternal Light, to July 28 and 29, 2009, when the PMOI in Ashraf, Iraq, repelled the attack of [then-Iraqi Prime Minister Nouri] Maliki's mercenaries with their bare hands to Massoud Rajavi's flight to France from Tehran's First Fighter Airbase on July 29, 1981, they indicate one thing: the Iranian Resistance's history, filled with vital turning points and risky

> *The fact is that a young and rebellious generation has turned to the anti-regime fighting force, to the democratic alternative, and to the struggle to overthrow the regime.*

and costly decisions, has led the regime to this precarious state of desperation and put the resistance and the alternative in a position of maximum offense.

It is not without reason that the NCRI Chairman and all of you are targets of the regime's demonization campaigns and lies.

Dear friends,

The NCRI's capabilities and competencies have been proven because a series of fundamental issues about the fate of the people, the revolution, Iran, and Iranians have found their worthy answer in this alternative. With the existence of this alternative, the overthrow of the regime will result in peace, stability, unity, and territorial integrity.

The uprisings of the past few years have proven that Iranians, from Arab compatriots to Kurdish, Baluchi, Turkmen, Qashqai and Bakhtiari compatriots, are all part of the same body and are united against the enemy of Iran and Iranians, i.e. the religious dictatorship. The National Council of Resistance of Iran has emphasized the autonomy within the framework of an indivisible country and its territorial integrity.

Finally, this alternative, with its set of programs, plans, views, and especially with its leadership in the battle against religious dictatorship, provides both the answer to the problems of today's struggle and the solution to the problems of tomorrow's Iran.

Let us remember Dr. Hezarkhani, who said at the NCRI meeting held at this time last year:

"When the PMOI opened up the narrow horizon of resistance in its weighty global campaign against Khomeini, I clearly said and wrote that the PMOI had succeeded in extricating the mind of Iranian society from the Middle Ages and welcomed it into the present era."

Our many greetings to the Chairman of the NCRI, the architect and organizer of this Resistance, who, in these sensitive, complex, and complicated circumstances, has restarted his series of teachings in simple language, to educate the young generation, and has thus guaranteed the training of a flourishing, fighting, and forward-thinking generation.

The alternative presented in the form of the National Council of Resistance of Iran is the product of the people's hardships and sacrifices, and at the same time, it is the most vivid and concrete proof attesting that the Iranian people's victory is certain.

Victory is yours.

Global campaign against
the disgraceful treaty between
Belgium and the Iranian regime
to secure the release of the
regime's terrorist diplomats

On the fourth anniversary of the foiled plot to cause a great massacre at the Iranian Resistance's gathering in Villepinte near Paris, which led to the arrest and trial of the regime terrorist diplomat Assadollah Assadi and three Tehran mercenaries, reports of a shameful deal between the regime and the Belgian government to secure the release of Assadi surfaced on July 1, 2022.

Assadi has been sentenced to 20 years in prison, four years of which he has already served. Mehrdad Arefani was sentenced to 17 years, and Nasimeh Naami and Amir Saadouni were each sentenced to 18 years in prison. The three agents' Belgian citizenships and passports were also revoked.

Following the news, the Secretariat of the National Council of Resistance of Iran published a call by Mrs. Maryam Rajavi to her compatriots, lawyers, political figures and representatives of the Belgian Parliament and other parliaments in Europe to prevent the transfer of terrorist diplomats of the regime to Iran. Following this call, mass demonstrations and sit-ins were held by Iranians in most of the European capitals and Washington, D.C.. A large number of protest letters and statements were also sent by international institutions and personalities to Belgian authorities.

For example, on Thursday, July 14, 2022, a large demonstration was held in Brussels, which thousands of Iranians and a number of Belgian parliamentarians and other political figures attended. Also in attendance were representatives of the European Parliament, prominent lawyers and members and officials of NCRI committees. In a video message, Maryam Rajavi addressed the participants. The text of her remarks is printed in subsequent pages:

Maryam Rajavi s message to the Irannians demonstrantion in Brussels

The global campaign against the treaty granting immunity to religious fascism's terrorism

Fellow compatriots,

Supporters of the Iranian Resistance,

I salute you, the harbingers of Iran's freedom and the standard-bearers of the global campaign against the clerical regime's shameful treaty with the Belgian government.

A treaty, whose actual substance and name amount to granting impunity to the religious fascism's terrorism and to the mullahs, who were about to carry out a mass killing in Paris, marking the biggest terrorist incident in Europe.

However, with your round-the-clock efforts, you, and other conscientious people, particularly in the Parliament of Belgium and other countries, exposed the scandalous conspiracy internationally in a short period of time.

You exposed a decision that extends the greatest encouragement to terrorism and crime on European soil on the world stage.

For me, it was a reminder of the June 17 conspiracy. The solidarity of freedom-loving Iranians once again made it clear that wherever they are, Iranians are the same as they were 20 years ago and 40 years ago. They will not rest when freedom, democracy, and human rights are sacrificed, and justice and the rule of law are trampled upon.

When this shameful treaty became public, the Iranian Resistance's Leader Massoud Rajavi said on July 1, "It is an insult to humankind's conscience and intellect, especially the Iranian people, that the Intelligence Ministry's diplomat-terrorist can spend his sentence in the prison of the very people who had sent him on his mission in the first place. Toying with the Judiciary and Justice in Belgium must be prevented."

He also said, "Voting for the disgraceful deal and plan desired by a terrorist and murderous regime is tantamount to bowing to religious fascism and the executioners of the Iranian people. It is a betrayal of democracy and human rights."

Moreover, the campaign against appeasing the unbridled terrorism of the ruling mullahs, just like the campaign to expose their secret nuclear facilities and projects, is not only defending the Iranian people's highest interests but also is a great service to global peace and security, especially as it relates to bombing peaceful gatherings and protecting the lives and safety of the people of Europe.

A global front against appeasement

Indeed, you inspired a global front against this collusion:
Senator Bob Menendez, chair of the US Senate Foreign Relations Committee, announced, "A Belgium-Iran treaty must uphold Belgium's international obligations and cannot grant impunity to Assadollah Asadi or any other actor responsible for human rights violations and heinous acts of terrorism. Iran must be held to account for backing terrorism and taking hostages for leverage."
Senator Ted Cruz, a senior member of the Senate Foreign Relations Committee, called the treaty "perplexing." He said the US had cooperated in investigating the 2018 terrorist plot against a political gathering in Paris so that "convicted terrorists should be punished, not freed."
Prominent international jurists, including Professor Eric David, said, "Allowing Assadi to serve (in violation of the UNSC 1373

Resolution) the remainder of his 20-year sentence in Iran, the state, which was responsible for the attempted terrorist bombing, would make a mockery of the rule of law and foster further impunity for the Iranian government and its officials involved in terrorism and crimes against humanity."

Professor John Mather, the Senior Project Scientist for the James Webb Space Telescope, also pointed out that this "unethical and scandalous treaty" would make "a mockery of the rule of law" and defeat "the world's efforts to fight terrorism."

And Professor Richard Roberts and other Nobel Laureates declared that the treaty would "set a dangerous precedent."

It must not be left untold that the Belgian Judiciary and its law enforcement officers did their job correctly and meticulously.

Parliamentary groups from different countries, as well as prominent European and American dignitaries such as Judge Michael Mukasey, former US Attorney General; Gen. James Jones, former National Security Advisor to US President; and Judge Louis Freeh, former director of the FBI, wrote in this regard, "This pending treaty is totally disrespectful to the law enforcement officers who risked their lives to prevent the 2018 attack."

The mullahs' hostage-taking tactic

In the face of Iranians' solidarity in Belgium, your campaign, and your global front, the advocates of appeasement and back-door deals have now turned the hostage-taking of Belgian citizens in Iran into a tactic against victims of terrorism.

In blatant sophistry, instead of blaming the hostage-takers and

> *The campaign against appeasing the unbridled terrorism of the ruling mullahs, just like the campaign to expose their secret nuclear facilities and projects, is not only defending the Iranian people's highest interests but also is a great service to global peace and security, especially as it relates to bombing peaceful gatherings and protecting the lives and safety of the people of Europe.*

adopting a stronger stance against the executioners, they want to appease them with the victims' blood. They say, what is wrong with sending a terrorist diplomat to a regime that sent him on a bombing mission? In return, they would free our hostage!

In this way, they fortify the theory of a "new type of power."

After the fatwa to kill Salman Rushdie, Javad Larijani, the human rights secretary of the mullahs' Judiciary, wrote a piece entitled, "A new type of power," in which he said: "Until now, the prevalent thinking was that political power should be defined based on military and economic power… However, the fatwa by Imam (Khomeini) showed that the source of political power is something else. The main source of power is to impact people's will."

The main issue for religious fascism ruling Iran is breaking the universal will against terrorism in Belgium and across Europe.

Pinning hope on the release of a Belgian hostage in Iran is one-step forward and 100 steps back because, in the future, no one will be safe. Every European and American citizen in Iran is also a potential hostage.

What must be done?

Indeed, what must be done?

The Iranian Resistance has already answered this question.

Seventy days ago, Massoud Rajavi said, "The Swedish government must confront the regime's extortion and blackmail (in the case of Ahmadreza Jalali) by immediately launching the prosecution of Raisi, the henchman of 1988, for committing crimes against humanity, war crimes, and genocide."

The Belgian government should have done and should do the same.

Indeed, what will you do if tomorrow, the mullahs blackmail all the people of Europe with the threat of a nuclear bomb?

Is it right to kneel and surrender? Where are the lessons and experiences of appeasing and going to war against Hitler, the Holocaust, and the gas chambers?

The regime's overthrow and the establishment of democracy and people's sovereignty are the tasks of the Iranian people and the Iranian Resistance. We have never asked this from anyone else, and we never will.

But since half a century ago, from the time of the Shah, we have asked to not take sides with dictatorship because overthrowing religious fascism is inevitable.

I thank my fellow compatriots, particularly university professors, specialists, athletes, artists, and Iranian political groups. I am also grateful to members of parliaments, jurists, dignitaries, and political parties, who joined this campaign, especially in Belgium and in its parliament. Their persistence against auctioneering values and the rule of law shows that the conscience of humanity is awake.

I extend my sincere gratitude to the Belgian judges for their endeavors to investigate the case of the regime's terrorist diplomat and vote for his conviction. I also thank members of the Parliament of Belgium for their brave opposition to the mullahs' disgraceful treaty.

So far, your campaign and the campaign of supporters of the Iranian Resistance has proven that when a people and their Resistance are vigilant and prepared,

when they quickly rush to the battlefield to defend the their people's freedom and liberty, they can turn the situation into their favor. And indeed, you are the extension of Iranian protesters and the Resistance Units on the international scene.

The fight will continue in all political, international, and legal arenas.

I urge all my compatriots to assist us in this endeavor.

Our guiding principle is relying on ourselves.

I say with deep conviction that when you tirelessly exhaust all options and do not give up, you will definitely win victory.

*Maryam Rajavi's message to the demonstration
of freedom-loving Iranians in Stockholm*

Sentencing one of the regime's perpetrators to life imprisonment in a court in Stockholm

On July 14, 2022, after 92 court sessions, a court in Stockholm convicted Hamid Noury, one of the perpetrators involved in genocide and crimes against humanity in Iran in 1988. The court handed down the most severe allowable punishment, sentencing Noury to life imprisonment. In a statement, Mrs. Rajavi welcomed the Swedish court's ruling.

To highlight this ruling, on July 16, freedom-loving Iranians and families of martyrs staged a large rally in Stockholm. Participants underscored the imperative to put on trial regime Supreme Leader Ali Khamenei, its President Ebrahim Raisi, Judiciary Chief Gholam-Hossein Ejei, and other officials involved in the 1988 massacre for committing genocide and crimes against humanity. A number of members of the Swedish Parliament, the MEK's lawyers, several political figures, and NCRI members spoke at the rally. The gathering commenced with participants viewing a video message addressed to the rally by Mrs. Maryam Rajavi.

We will continue the Call for Justice Movement with maximum determination

Fellow compatriots,

Dear friends and supporters of the Iranian Resistance,

I salute and congratulate you all for staying loyal to your pledges with the 1988 massacre martyrs and always being prepared to preserve the PMOI/MEK's traditions, ideology, and leader.

You stay your ground against whoever wants to trample upon the blood of PMOI martyrs and the movement seeking justice for them to the benefit of the clerical regime.

Indeed, what you did over the past year is yet another roaring epic.

May your determination and struggle in the fight against the clerical regime be forever enduring.

Prosecution of Khamenei and Raisi

After nearly three years, the Swedish Judiciary handed down its verdict, sentencing to life one of the perpetrators of genocide and crime against humanity in the massacre of political prisoners in 1988. And I stress this is only one out of all the murderers involved.

Of course, we welcome the ruling, which is the outcome of your efforts and sacrifices and deserves to be congratulated. However, full justice will be only done when all the masterminds and perpetrators are prosecuted in the Iranian people's courts. That includes Ali Khamenei, Ebrahim Raisi, Hossein-Ali Nayeri, Gholam-Hossein Mohseni Ejei, and others.

Also, the mercenaries and operatives whose collaboration with the regime Amnesty International has documented.

The Death Commission made PMOI prisoners answer the following questions:

-Are you ready to condemn the PMOI/MEK and its leaders?

-Are you ready to join the armed forces of the Islamic Republic to fight the PMOI/MEK?

-Are you willing to spy on your former comrades and cooperate with intelligence agents?

-Are you willing to become a member of the death squads?

-Are you ready to hang a PMOI prisoner?

Yes, in the Iranian people's ultimate call for justice, the secrets of the biggest massacre of political prisoners in contemporary history will be revealed. The questions that Massoud Rajavi asked the UN Human Rights Rapporteur on February 12, 1996, will also be answered.

- What is the exact number of political prisoners executed during the massacre and before and after it?

-Where are the bodies buried?

-Where are the mass graves?

-How many of those executed were under 18?

-How many of them were women, especially teenage girls?

-And the number and addresses of official and unofficial prisons and safe houses of the Intelligence Ministry, the IRGC, and the State Security Force.

In the past years and months, you, the steadfast supporters of the Iranian Resistance, showed that you are ready to do everything to make this great day come true. You arc prepared to pay any price in unison and in solidarity with the Resistance Units inside Iran.

The PMOI face-off with the clerical regime

The story of the 1988 massacre is the story of an inhuman regime's confrontation with its only existential threat, i.e., the People's Mojahedin Organization of Iran (PMOI/MEK).

Khomeini's fatwa for the massacre remains the main criterion for the regime's conduct vis-à-vis the PMOI and the Iranian Resistance.

The physical, political, and ideological elimination of the PMOI/MEK topped the clerical regime's agenda from the first year.

We just recently heard this fact from Hossein-Ali Nayeri, the head of the Death Commission in Tehran. He explicitly said, "If it were not for the decisiveness of Imam (Khomeini), we might not have had any security… The whole system would not have survived. What should have been done? Such critical circumstances deemed a decisive fatwa."

Nayeri also revealed the regime's desperation in the face of the prisoners who remained steadfast. He said, "They were cohesive. Not only did they have contact with their organization, but they also had formed a new organizational structure inside the prison. They received information from outside through ways they knew. They dominated the prison's atmosphere. So, they wanted to continue their hostility."

This criminal thus acknowledges the very truth that the court's witnesses and plaintiffs said about the courage of PMOI prisoners, who fully cognizant, adhered to their principles and beliefs and said "NO" to Khomeini and his operatives. They remained loyal to the name, the path, and the cause championed by the PMOI and Massoud Rajavi and kissed the noose.

Of course, the case examined in this court was a small part of what happened in Gohardasht Prison.

You can imagine the day when the heinous massacre in Evin and

> *In the Iranian people's ultimate call for justice, the secrets of the biggest massacre of political prisoners in contemporary history will be revealed.*
> *- What is the exact number of political prisoners executed during the massacre and before and after it?*
> *-Where are the bodies buried?*
> *-Where are the mass graves?*
> *-How many of those executed were under 18?*
> *-How many of them were women, especially teenage girls?*

the countless crimes committed in various cities will be revealed. You can imagine the day when the heroism of female PMOI prisoners during the massacre and the crimes committed against them will be revealed.

Dear friends, sisters, and brothers,

We still have a long way ahead of us before we achieve complete justice. But the Iranian Resistance's extensive legal, political, and enlightening campaign over the past 33 months has already achieved a great victory so far. And you had an indispensable role in this victory.

The court's ruling has crushed the multi-dimensional plot by the Intelligence Ministry and its mercenaries to derail the Call for Justice Movement against the PMOI/MEK.

Their plot included the necessary preparations to have Hamid Noury acquitted and released.

You certainly recall the statement of the NCRI's Security and Counter-terrorism Committee on November 15, 2019, which exposed this plot. The statement said, "Dozens of PMOI members at Ashraf-3 (who have witnessed Hamid Noury's crimes first-hand) are ready to testify about what they saw.

However, any meaningful judicial investigation of Hamid Noury's case, free of wheeling and dealing, requires halting the involvement of the regime's agents in this case."

The trial would have turned out differently if some of the court sessions had not been held in Albania. The court was presented with decisive documents proving Noury's guilt to which the prosecutor repeatedly referred.

Perseverance of the Iranian Resistance's supporters

Your unrelenting nine-month demonstrations outside the Court in Stockholm had an unforgettable role in this great campaign.

You stood firm despite the freezing temperatures to defend the identity and cause of the martyrs of the 1988 massacre. You did not allow the regime, its agents and mercenaries distort and cover up the real objective of the Call for Justice Movement.

Let's not forget that this case still has many serious questions and

ambiguities that need to be addressed and answered.

The NCRI Security and Counter-terrorism and the Judiciary committees have pointed out these instances. There is no doubt that truth will come out.

In 2016, with the completion of PMOI's relocation from Camp Liberty (Iraq) to Albania, we gave urgent priority and extra resources to the case of the massacre of 1988.

I have repeatedly declared that we will continue the Call for Justice Movement with maximum determination. I reiterated that we would not relent until we pour the poison chalice of human rights down the throat of religious fascism just as we forced the regime to drink the poison chalice of ceasefire (in the Iran-Iraq war). Now, we have taken one step forward in the path to Call for Justice Movement. However, it must continue until all the regime's leaders and officials face justice.

I want to be clear: Genocide, crime against humanity, and massacre must be recognized - with precisely these legal terms-- by national and international courts and the UN Security Council. And international investigation must be carried out in the presence of the representatives of the Iranian Resistance.

The Iranian people's fight against the clerical regime and the Resistance movement that started on June 20, 1981, independent from any foreign government or power, will forge ahead with full power until we overthrow the mullahs as desired by the Iranian people.

I salute you for standing up and changing the equations. You will continue and you will stand to the end, strong and steadfast, and loyal to your pledges. Onward to greater victories,
Victory is yours.

US Secretary of State

Mike Pompeo's visit to Ashraf-3

Maryam Rajavi's meeting with Secretary Mike Pompeo

US Secretary of State Mike Pompeo, who left the post in January 2021, visited Albania for the first time and met and talked with Mrs. Maryam Rajavi at Ashraf-3 in the afternoon of Monday, May 16, 2022.

Mr. Pompeo visited the Resistance's museum in Ashraf 3, which depicts parts of the struggle and resistance of the Iranian people in the past century against the dictatorships of the Shah and the mullahs for a free Iran and a democratic republic. He also signed the memorial book at this museum.

During his visit to Ashraf-3, Mr. Pompeo visited different parts of the Resistance museum, including areas related to popular uprisings, Resistance Units, massacre of political prisoners, the regime's medieval torture chambers, the symbolic cells of Evin and Qezel Hesar prisons, as well as life-sized models of the Death Corridor and the Execution Hall at Gohardasht prison, all of which have been reconstructed in the Resistance museum.

Pompeo visits
The Resistance's museum in Ashraf 3

Paying tribute to 30,000 heroes executed
during the massacre of 1988

Mike Pompeo speaks at the gathering of MEK to Ashraf-3

Secretary Pompeo attended and addressed a gathering of thousands of members of the PMOI. In parts of his speech, he said:

... Over 1000 former political prisoners of the theocratic regime are gathered here today. I want to say to you, from a former Secretary of State, that America recognizes and deeply respects you. The things you have suffered in the name of freedom reminds us of what our country was founded to defend and secure so many years ago.

It is an honor to be with you. I'd also like to recognize President-elect Maryam Rajavi. Under her leadership, the National Council of Resistance of Iran is laying the groundwork for a free, sovereign, and democratic republic in Iran. Bless you, madam.

Maryam Rajavi:
The Iranian people and the organized Resistance are the decisive factors in developments pertaining to Iran

Maryam Rajavi addressed and welcomed Secretary Pompeo. The following is the text of her remarks:

Mr. Secretary,

Welcome to Ashraf-3, home to the Iranian people's Resistance. Those here today continue the Iranian people's 120-year-long struggle for freedom. They include 1,000 tortured political prisoners during the Shah's dictatorship and those imprisoned under the mullahs' tyranny.

We can and must liberate Iran, the Middle East, and the world from the evil nuclear mullahs

In visiting the Resistance's Museum, you saw a glimpse of the Iranian people's enormous pain and suffering on the one hand and their struggle for freedom, on the other.

The Iranian people and the mullahs' regime have faced off ferociously in the past 43 years. And this fight will continue until a free democratic republic is established in Iran.

For a while, the mullahs tried to portray Iraq as the enemy. Then, they tried to portray the United States as the enemy. But the people of Iran and the MEK say that our enemy is in Iran.

The mullahs said the MEK were terrorists, a cult, and the enemies of God. They claimed the MEK did not have any base of support in Iran. There are many similar and baseless allegations.

There are two significant factors to the conflict in today's Iran: On the one hand, we see the regime at its weakest point. On the other, we see the people's maximum anger and discontent. The outcome of these factors has been the progress and expansion of the organized Resistance.

The West ignored the Iranian people and their organized resistance as the decisive factor in the developments pertaining to Iran for four decades. It thus enabled the mullahs such that they are on the verge of having a nuclear bomb.

As you said last September, you are "on the right side of this fight." You said, and I quote, "Iran will never return to rule by a dictatorial Shah or theocratic regime. The central fight is the one in the streets, and in the mosques, and in the minds of the Iranian people - it is the divide between the people and the organized opposition seeking freedom and democracy on one side and the entirety of the regime on the other. I have been in this fight on the right side for over a decade now."

These days the price of the bread has multiplied. Thus, Iranian cities are rising one after the other against the mullahs' regime.

> ***The West ignored the Iranian people and their organized resistance as the decisive factor in the developments pertaining to Iran for four decades. It thus enabled the mullahs such that they are on the verge of having a nuclear bomb.***

Appeasement or decisiveness?

By glancing at the objective conditions and the successive eruption of uprisings in Iran, today one can see that regime change is on the horizon. The people of Iran have already decided to engage in the final confrontation with the regime.

In January 2019, you said, "We must confront the ayatollahs, not coddle them."

Appeasement or decisiveness, siding with the ruling dictators or with the people? This has been the major challenge of Iran policy over the past four decades.

The outcome of appeasing the ruling religious fascism has been the five-capital strategy, which you mentioned three and a half years ago, by referring to the situations in Iraq, Syria, Lebanon, and Yemen.

We have always insisted that appeasement and offering concessions will not contain the regime nor change its behavior. Instead, it will only provide the mullahs with opportunity and motivation to pursue their destructive policies.

Four years ago, around this time, you correctly set 12 conditions the regime had to meet to change its behavior. But the world saw that the mullahs did not accept even one of the 12 even when a so-called moderate government was in office.

The West has consistently ignored the role of the Iranian people and Resistance when formulating its policy vis-à-vis Iran. This void explains why the West was caught by surprise during the 1979 Revolution that toppled the Shah.

The Shah resorted to mass killings and martial law in the final months of his rule, but it had the opposite effect. Likewise, Khamenei appointed Ebrahim Raisi, an executioner implicated in the massacre of political prisoners, as his regime's president, to close ranks in the face of the uprisings and save his regime.

After one year, one can certainly say that Khamenei's dream did not come true. The regime is in a deadlock and has no future but inevitable downfall.

Therefore, the regime has found the only solution in trying to eliminate the organized Resistance and its only democratic alternative through suppression, terrorism, and the demonization campaigns. It even claims that no alternative to the regime exists. The mullahs' criminal regime has included you among its terrorism targets. In my view, this reflects the veracity and importance of your positions. It is a badge of honor for anyone to be targeted by the religious fascism.

Of course, the mullahs will take these dreams to their graves.

Aspirations of the Iranian people's Resistance

A few days ago, the Court of Appeals in Antwerp, Belgium, convicted three agents of the Iranian Intelligence Ministry for attempting to bomb the Iranian Resistance's annual gathering in Paris.

They acted under the command of a diplomat-terrorist who had already been sentenced to 20 years in prison.

This act of state terrorism before anything else shows the regime's fear of the Iranian Resistance and its democratic alternative.

After the Court of Antwerp ruling, we urged the EU to cut diplomatic ties with Tehran. The experience of the past 40 years has shown that this regime does not understand any language but the language of firmness and force.

To this end, the Resistance Units have expanded across the country. Over the last Persian year, they carried out more than 2,230 anti-repression campaigns to pave the way for uprisings.

Since January, the Resistance Units have carried out several major campaigns disrupting the operations of the state-run national radio and television networks, its ministry of propaganda, and the ministry that plunders Iranian farmers.

In addition, since Thursday, the Iranian Resistance has made public valuable information it has obtained from within the regime's Prisons Organization.

The Iranian Resistance exposed the regime's secret nuclear and missile sites 20 years ago and alerted the world. Otherwise, the mullahs would have already obtained the atomic bomb.

Today, we warn again that one should not delay.

We say that we can and must free Iran, the Middle East, and

the world of the evil of the nuclear mullahs. First, by imposing comprehensive sanctions and international isolation of the religious dictatorship. The mullahs' regime should be placed under Article 41 of Chapter 7 of the UN Charter;

Second, by referring the dossier of human rights abuses in Iran and the clerical regime's terrorism to the UN Security Council, particularly the files on the massacre of 30,000 political prisoners in 1988 and the killing of 1,500 during the November 2019 uprising;

Third, by recognizing the struggle of Iran's rebellious youths against the IRGC and the struggle of the entire Iranian nation to overthrow the mullahs' regime.

And finally, as you said, "In the end, the Iranian people will have a secular, democratic, non-nuclear Republic."

> *By glancing at the objective conditions and the successive eruption of uprisings in Iran, today one can see that regime change is on the horizon. The people of Iran have already decided to engage in the final confrontation with the regime.*

Mike Pence's visit
to Ashraf 3

Vice President Mike Pence and Mrs. Karen Pence meet Mrs. Maryam Rajavi

Mike Pence, the US Vice President until 2021, met and held talks with Maryam Rajavi at Ashraf-3 on June 23, 2022.

Mrs. Karen Pence, and Mr. Marc Short, the former director of legislative affairs in the White House until 2021 and chief of staff to Vice President Mike Pence, accompanied Mr. Pence. He visited the Resistance's Museum at Ashraf-3 and addressed a PMOI/MEK gathering.

At the PMOI/MEK gathering, Maryam Rajavi welcomed Mr. Pence. She said in her remarks, "One thousand political prisoners tortured by the Shah's regime or the ruling religious dictatorship are present in this hall today. Some have lost 10 or 12 family members. The Iranian Resistance set a historical example: the resistance of a nation can change the course of history towards freedom."

Maryam Rajavi underscored that the Iranian regime's dossier on human rights violations and terrorism, particularly the massacre of political prisoners in 1988, and the crackdown on protesters in November 2019, must be referred to the UN Security Council, and the regime's leaders must be prosecuted for committing genocide and crimes against humanity.

Visiting the Musum of the Resistance in Ashraf3

Paying tribute to 30,000 heroes executed during the massacre of 1988

Vice President Mike Pence addressed a PMOI/MEK gathering

Vice President Mike Pence attended and addressed a gathering of thousands of members of the PMOI. In parts of his speech, he said:

... "I have traveled more than 5,000 miles from my home in Indiana to be here today because we share a common cause: the liberation of the Iranian people from decades of tyranny, and the rebirth of a free, peaceful, prosperous, and democratic Iran. Thank you all for standing strong in the name of freedom," Vice President Pence stated."

"Today we call on the Biden administration to immediately withdraw from all nuclear negotiations with Tehran, voice support for the organized opposition in Iran, and make it clear that the United States and our allies will never allow Iran to obtain nuclear weapons."

"I can say with certainty that the American people are with you as you stand and labor for freedom in Iran. The American people support your goal of establishing a secular, democratic, non-nuclear Iranian republic that derives its just powers from the consent of the governed."

"Today, I join you in pledging that his crimes must not go unpunished. Ebrahim Raisi is unworthy of leading the great people of Iran. He must be removed from office by the people of Iran – and he must be prosecuted for crimes against humanity and genocide that he perpetrated thirty years ago and every day since."

"Today, the resistance movement in Iran has never been stronger. It's been inspiring for me today to learn more. Resistance Units in Iran are the center of hope for the Iranian people. They are an engine for change from within during the uprisings and continued protests. And every day, it's clear they are growing stronger while the regime grows weaker."

"Your Resistance Units, commitment to democracy, human rights, and freedom for every citizen of Iran. Maryam Rajavi's Ten Point Plan for the future of Iran will ensure freedom of expression, freedom of assembly, and the freedom for every Iranian to choose their elected leaders."

"The regime in Tehran wants to trick the world into believing that the Iranian protesters want to return to the dictatorship of the Shah as well. But we are not confused by their lies."

"The day will come when the ayatollahs release their iron-fisted grip on Iran and her people. A new glorious day will dawn, and a bright future will begin, ushering in an era of peace, prosperity, stability, and freedom for the good people of Iran and the world," Vice President Mike Pence concluded.

Maryam Rajavi: The Iranian Resistance is the key to freedom and democracy

Speech to the MEK gathering hosting Mike Pence, the 48th US Vice President

Mr. Vice President and Mrs. Pence,

Welcome to Ashraf-3, home to the Iranian people's Resistance.

I want to begin with recalling a memory from Ashraf in Iraq. During the attacks on Ashraf on July 28 and 29, 2009, we had 13 martyrs and 505 wounded. Most of those injured are here in this hall.

Two days after the deadly attack, the friends of the Iranian Resistance in US Congress tabled House Resolution 704, that garnered a bipartisan majority. The resolution strongly condemned

> *Today, I want to underscore three points: First, the objective conditions of Iranian society; second, the alternative to the regime; and third, the international community's approach to the religious fascism ruling Iran.*

the massacre of Ashraf residents, and demanded safeguards for their well-being.

The resolution urged the US President to "take all necessary and appropriate steps to support the commitments of the United States under international law and treaty obligations to ensure the physical security and protection of Camp Ashraf residents."

I only mention the names of a few of the signatories to that resolution:

Congressman Mike Pence, a Republican Party leader and a member of the Foreign Affairs Committee;

The late Congressman John Lewis, Representatives Ed Towns, and Sheila Jackson Lee from the Democratic Party; Judge Ted Poe, Dana Rohrabacher, and Iliana Ros-Lehtinen from the Republican Party.

And today, after 13 years, on behalf of all Ashraf residents, I would like to say, thank you, Mr. Vice President and I also thank your colleagues for stopping that carnage.

Your visit to Ashraf-3 coincides with the Iranian people's uprisings. Various sectors of our nation have risen up in different cities, including Tehran, Ahvaz, Isfahan, Shush, Zanjan and Rasht.The Resistance Units are also fighting across the country.

Three days ago, marked the beginning of the 42nd year of our nationwide Resistance against the mullahs' regime.

On June 20, 1981, Khomeini ordered his Revolutionary Guards to open fire on the MEK's half-a-million-strong and peaceful demonstration in Tehran, and turned it into a mass killing.

The same night, mass executions began without even identifying the victims.

Moments ago, in the Museum of Resistance, you saw a glimpse of the Iranian people's suffering under the mullahs' rule and also their resistance against the regime. One thousand political prisoners tortured by the Shah's regime or the ruling religious dictatorship are present in this hall today. Some have lost 10 or 12 family members.

You know about Khomeini's fatwa for the execution of all MEK members and sympathizers, who remained steadfast in their ideal. This, no doubt, is evidence of a strong and relentless resistance to establish a free and democratic Iran.

You rightly said last October in Washington that, "The atrocity of 1988, the fatwa that was issued by the Ayatollah, resulting in the murder of 30,000 members of the MEK, was ultimately about religion and a belief that people who believed in liberty and in freedom for Iran did not have the religion that was acceptable to the tyrants in Tehran."

The MEK is also proud of stopping Khomeini's expansionist war in 1988. He had been waging that conflict for eight years with the slogan of liberating Quds (Jerusalem) via Karbala.

However, in 1988, the National Liberation Army of Iran forced Khomeini, to, in his own words, drink the chalice of the poison of the ceasefire in a war with one million dead, two million maimed and wounded, 4 million homeless, and more than one trillion dollars in damages on the Iranian side alone.

> *Our Islam rejects tyranny and misogyny. It respects and guarantees the rights of oppressed ethnic minorities. It does not distinguish between the ways of Christ, the ways of Moses, and the ways of Muhammad.*
> *By promoting the separation of religion and state, this alternative is a solution to establish democracy in Iran and an obstacle to Islamic fundamentalism in the entire region.*

The MEK was also the first to expose the regime's nuclear projects since 1991. In 2002, it uncovered the regime's secret sites and informed the world of its bomb-making program.

Without those revelations, the mullahs would have obtained the bomb years ago.

Iranian society is ready for change

Today, I want to underscore three points: First, the objective conditions of Iranian society; second, the alternative to the regime; and third, the international community's approach to the religious fascism ruling Iran.

First, the world is witnessing that conditions are ripe for change in Iran and that people are ready for change.

Protests are erupting with increasing intensity across the country. On the other hand, the regime has no answer except stepping up repression, executions or torture in its prisons. The people of Iran have the right to resist, much like the war of independence in America. The mullahs have occupied our country. People now chant, "Our enemy is right here; they lie when they say it's America."

The Iranian Resistance set a historical example: the resistance of a nation can change the course of history towards freedom.

Today, we see this experience in Ukraine. Indeed, if the people of Ukraine themselves had not taken up arms, what would have guaranteed the protection of their country?

External conditions are effective only when a fighting force on the ground is prepared to pay the price.

In the past year, the MEK Resistance Units in Iran carried out more than 2,350 campaigns against repression that paved the way for uprisings across our nation.

Second, by virtue of believing in a democratic Islam, the MEK is an effective counterforce to the mullahs' sinister ideology. Look at what the mullahs have done in the name of Islam in Iran's neighboring countries, from Iraq to Syria, to Lebanon, Palestine, and Yemen.

But our Islam rejects tyranny and misogyny. It respects and guarantees the rights of oppressed ethnic minorities. It does not distinguish between the ways of Christ, the ways of Moses, and the ways of Muhammad.

By promoting the separation of religion and state, this alternative is a solution to establish democracy in Iran and an obstacle to Islamic fundamentalism in the entire region.

The mullahs' regime has made every effort to cover-up this truth. Demonizing the Iranian Resistance, censoring its news, and denying its popular support arc all intended to cover-up the truth.

Now that all illusions about any reform within the regime in Iran have disappeared, the mullahs are investing on a non-existent Shah to divert the uprisings.

But you rightly said, "I'm confident I speak for the views of tens of millions of Americans. And I tell you with certainty that the American people support your goal of establishing a democratic, secular, non-nuclear Iranian Republic."

Yes, Tehran rulers are at their weakest point. They face the Iranian people's uprisings for change.

We can and must rid Iran, the Middle East, and the world from the evil of nuclear mullahs.

The November 2019 uprising, with its rebellious cities and the Army of freedom, showed the way.

Third, today, the world clearly sees that the policy of appeasement of the mullahs has failed.

This is a regime that gives a bomb to its diplomat to blow up the gathering of the Iranian Resistance where hundreds of distinguished international personalities were present.

The Iranian people and Resistance deserve international recognition and support

This is a regime that disables IAEA cameras at its nuclear sites and runs more advanced centrifuges.

Yes, this regime has never abandoned its quest for nuclear weapons as a guarantee for its survival. This is part of Raisi's mission.

The International Community must activate the trigger mechanism. The Iranian regime's dossier on human rights violations and terrorism, particularly the massacre of political prisoners in 1988, and the crackdown on protesters in November 2019, must be referred to the UN Security Council, and the regime's leaders must be prosecuted for committing genocide and crimes against humanity.

If the regime did not intend to provoke wars, its conventional army would have sufficed. Therefore, the Revolutionary Guard Corps (the IRGC) must be dismantled.

Like Ukraine, the Iranian people and their Resistance deserve international recognition and support. The war of Iran's rebellious youths against the terrorist IRGC to overthrow the regime must be recognized.

Mr. Vice President and Mrs. Pence,

Today, Iran's freedom fighters who have fought against the Shah's regime and the religious tyranny ruling our nation welcomed you to Ashraf-3.Tomorrow, a free Iran will welcome you for standing by the Iranian people and Resistance.

Thank you and God bless you.

Sir Richard Roberts, Nobel Laureate in medicine and Maryam Rajavi meet at Ashraf-3

Professor Richard Roberts, 1993 Nobel Laureate in medicine, and Maryam Rajavi met and held talks in Ashraf-3 on Sunday, June 26, 2022.

Mr. Roberts also visited the Resistance's Museum and addressed a gathering of PMOI members in Ashraf-3.

Professor Richard Roberts is a valuable scholar of molecular biology. His research led to the discovery of alternative splicing of genes, which proved instrumental in the prevention, and treatment of hereditary illnesses in infants.

The Nobel Committee gave the 1993 Nobel Prize in medicine to Professor Roberts for his discovery.

Professor Roberts is also a humanitarian scientist who has repeatedly protested and issued declarations against the crackdowns on the PMOI in Ashraf and Liberty, and the massacre of 30,000 political prisoners in Iran in joint action with other Nobel Laureates.

During the Iranian people's uprising in 2009, he sponsored a letter to the UN Secretary-General to condemn the slaughter of protesters.

Maryam Rajavi and MEK welcoming Prof. Roberts

Professor Richard Roberts among MEK members at Ashraf-3:

"The Resistance Museum was an amazing experience and it should be made more widely available to the rest of the world. My firm hope after today's visit to the museum is that in the not so distant future, I will be able to meet all of you in Tehran."

Maryam Rajavi:
Scientists defending Iranian people's Resistance are beacons of the worlds' scientific community

Maryam Rajavi's speech in the presence of the Nobel Laureate in medicine Prof. Roberts

Dear Professor Roberts,Distinguished scientist and pioneer,
Dear friend of the Iranian people and Resistance
Welcome to Ashraf-3, home of the Iranian people's freedom.
It is an honor for me and all the freedom fighters, for the MEK members -- jailed and tortured by the religious and monarchical dictatorships-present here right now, and for the Iranian Resistance, that you visited Ashraf-3. We are delighted to welcome you here. We and the Iranian people will remember this visit because of your distinguished scientific career,
because of your support for the Iranian people's uprisings for freedom,
and particularly because of your sincere and heartfelt defense of the MEK in Ashraf and Liberty during the seven years, from 2009 until 2016, where 150 MEK members were slain and nearly 1,500 wounded in seven bloodbaths. From the first attack until today, you have acted 22 times in support of Iran's freedom fighters and the Iranian people's protests.
I salute you and your colleagues, the other Nobel laureates, who joined you in this tremendous campaign.
The history of science and freedom will never forget such

> *For years, our Resistance has been subjected to a demonization campaign to force it to abandon its beliefs and positions and accept that freedom will never come.*
> *But we have pledged to make freedom flourish throughout Iran with our body and soul!*

scientists and will etch their names with gold in its annals. Science and freedom are the two sides of the same coin that seeks the liberation of the human race from determinism, blind destiny, and restrictive social compulsions.

Indeed, in our era, you, Professor Roberts and dozens of other Nobel Laureates are the pioneers and trailblazers in this path.

You are the beacon for other scholars and scientists at a time when oppressive dictatorships trampled on human values, and when freedom fighters endured greatest pressures and most brutal tortures for the longest times.

Fighting for a democratic society

The 57-year history of the MEK has been the story of a relentless struggle against monarchical and religious dictatorships to achieve freedom and democracy for their people.

Since 120 years ago, the people of Iran have risen upfor freedom and democracy. Overturning the dictatorships of Shah and the mullahs to establish a democratic and an advanced society has constituted the objective of our people's struggle.

For the greater part of this era, namely since 57 years ago, the People's Mojahedin Organization of Iran (PMOI/MEK) has been at the center of the resistance movement, which has introduced a democratic alternative to the ruling theocracy. At the same time, it has created a living model of the separation of religion and state and gender equality.

In the first decade of this century, the MEK was under the siege of two dictatorships in Ashraf City in Iraq, enduring the heaviest pressures for 10 years. They persevered in the face of relentless suppression aimed at genocide and annihilating the MEK.

When Khamenei's puppet government in Iraq attacked Ashraf residents, you and and a stellar roster of other freedom-loving scientists and elites around the world wrote to the UN Secretary-General, the US government, the European Union, MPs and officials of various countries. You lent your scientific credentials and international prestige to defend the Iranian Resistance movement.

Iran, the global record holder in brain drain

Our country was once the cradle of worlds' most renowned scientists, including Jabir Ibn Hayyan, Seyyed Esmaeil Jorjani, Abu Rayhan Al-Biruni, Avicenna, Abu Bakr al-Razi, Omar Khayyam, Abu Nasr Al-Farabi, Khajeh Nasir al-Din Toosi, and Muhammad Khawrizmi. They were among the most outstanding scientists in physics, chemistry, astronomy, medicine, mathematics, and natural sciences in previous centuries.

But repression, liberticide, and widespread plundering of the people's property by the ruling religious fascism has no limits. Today, Iran holds the world record for brain drain. In the last three years alone, about 4,000 doctors and 300,000 specialists with masters and doctorate degrees, including 900 university professors, have left Iran.

When Khomeini seized power in Iran, universities were the main headquarters of the People's Mojahedin. At that time, Massoud Rajavi [the leader of the Resistance] was teaching philosophy at Sharif University of Technology under the title "Explaining the World." Some 10,000 students attended this weekly course. And the text of the courses was immediately copied and distributed on a large scale to other universities and to MEK supporters.

But Khomeini could not tolerate it. Fourteen months after coming to power in April 1980, Khomeini launched a brutal crackdown on universities on the pretext of a Cultural Revolution. By April 22, 1980, at least 17 students had been killed and 2,180 injured. Massoud Rajavi's classes were also shut down, afterwards.

On March 29, 1980, Le Monde reported that tens of thousands of students carrying admission cards attended Massoud Rajavi's comparative philosophy courses every Friday afternoon . The text of these courses were sold as paperback in hundreds of thousands of copies, and about 100,000 students would watch their video recording in 35 major cities of Iran.

Le Monde wrote that as a popular party, the MEK was one of the best-organized organizations in Iran. According to various political commentators, had Khomeini not vetoed Massoud Rajavi's candidacy during the presidential election by issuing a fatwa, he would have won several million votesand garnered the support of ethnic and religious minorities, and a large segment of women and young people, who rejected the reactionary clerics' supremacy.

So, Khomeini launched a bloody crackdown on universities and colleges and closed them down, calling this coup against culture a "cultural revolution!"

At that time, Khomeini said, "We are not afraid of economic blockade, military intervention, or (in his words) colonial university. Our universities are not beneficial for our nation. I support the decision made by the Revolutionary Council and the president to purge the university."

Interestingly, when universities reopened two or three years after the so-called Cultural Revolution, they were governed by the laws of religious fascism. More than 40% of university admissions were allocated to the regime's security forces, such as the paramilitary Bassij and the Revolutionary Guard Corps (IRGC), and those who conducted the unpatriotic war against Iraq.

Even today, universities and students are subject to severe repression and control. Many university professors live in

poverty. The regime has executed tens of thousands of students and teachers. Currently, teachers are imprisoned for protesting against their meager salaries.

The mullahs impose the reactionary laws of the previous millennia on the people to govern the society, including those related to legal and judicial matters. But they use the latest sci-entific and technological advances to preserve their decadent rule and to build atomic bombs and missiles.

As Massoud [Rajavi] said: The mullahs "want to cover up the inherent poverty of a despond-ent regime on borrowed time, with enriched uranium and keep it in power.

"What kind of peaceful energy and science is this that it has been in the hands of Revolu-tionary Guards?

"Why has this so-called research been kept secret for two decades and, at the same time, devoured the money that should have been allocated to teachers, educators, universities, pensioners, and workers?"

Our pledge is to make freedom flourish throughout Iran

Prof. Roberts,

I want to share with you the story of another tragedy.

The massacre of political prisoners in 1988 is unique in the massive dossier of the regime's crimes. Khomeini issued a fatwa against the People's Mojahedin, stating that anyone who maintained his/her beliefs should be executed, namely those who remained steadfast in their belief in the freedom of their people and homeland and were unwilling to express remorse because of their organizational affiliation, ideals, and leadership. As such, 30,000 people were hanged, 90% from the MEK.

Quite a few doctors were among the countless martyrs, including Dr. Adel Malayeri, Dr. Farzin Nemati, Dr. Firouz Saremi, Dr. Hamideh Siyahi, and Dr. Nahid Sedighi .

In July 2021, you and a dozen of your colleagues wrote a letter to the UN Secretary-General calling for the formation of a fact-finding mission to investigate the 1988 massacre of political prisoners. In this letter, you underlined the role of the regime's president, Ebrahim Raisi, in commiting crimes against humanity. For years, our Resistance has been subjected to a demonization campaign to force it to abandon its beliefs and positions and accept that freedom will never come.

But we have pledged to make freedom flourish throughout Iran with our body and soul!

I think it is our shared belief that no force in the world can stop the progress of science and freedom.

In conclusion, I must add that we missed Dr. Sheikhi, Chair of the NCRI Universities' Committee, among us. I asked Dr. Sassan Mohaddess who had arranged Professor Roberts's visit. He said the arrangements had been done very quickly and there was no time to inform Dr. Sheikhi. At any rate, we reserve his place here next to Professor Roberts.

I thank you again for coming here.

Maryam Rajavi's Ten Point Plan for the future of Iran

1. Rejection of velayat-e faqih (absolute clerical rule). Affirmation of the people's sovereignty in a republic founded on universal suffrage and pluralism;

2. Freedom of speech, freedom of political parties, freedom of assembly, freedom of the press and the internet. Dissolution and disbanding of the Islamic Revolutionary Guard Corps (IRGC), the terrorist Qods Force, plainclothes groups, the unpopular Bassij, the Ministry of Intelligence, Council of the Cultural Revolution, and all suppressive patrols and institutions in cities, villages, schools, universities, offices, and factories;

3. Commitment to individual and social freedoms and rights in accordance with the Universal Declaration of Humans Rights. Disbanding all agencies in charge of censorship and inquisition. Seeking justice for massacred political prisoners, prohibition of torture, and the abolishment of the death penalty;

4. Separation of religion and state, and freedom of religions and faiths;

5. Complete gender equality in the realms of political, social, cultural, and economic rights, and equal participation of women in political leadership.

Abolishment of any form of discrimination; the right to choose one's own clothing freely; the right to freely marry and divorce, and to obtain education and employment. Prohibition of all forms of exploitation against women under any pretext;

6. An independent judiciary and legal system consistent with international standards based on the presumption of innocence, the right to defense counsel, right of appeal, and the right to be tried in a public court. Full independence of judges. Abolishment of the mullahs' Sharia law and dissolution of Islamic Revolutionary Courts;

7. Autonomy for and removal of double injustices against Iranian nationalities and ethnicities consistent with the NCRI's plan for the autonomy of Iranian Kurdistan;

8. Justice and equal opportunities in the realms of employment and entrepreneurship for all people of Iran in a free market economy. Restoration of the rights of blue-collar workers, farmers, nurses, white-collar workers, teachers, and retirees;

9. Protection and rehabilitation of the environment, which has been massacred under the rule of the mullahs; and

10. A non-nuclear Iran that is also devoid of weapons of mass destruction. Peace, co-existence, and international and regional cooperation.

Lists of several publications by the National Council of Resistance of Iran

Iran without Execution
Maryam Rajavi
October 2015

Tolerant Islam vs. Extremism
Maryam Rajavi
August 2016

**L'islam de la liberté
contre l'extrémisme et
l'obscurantisme**
Maryam Rajavi
August 2016

**No to Compulsory Veil,
No to Comulsory Religion,
No to Compulsory Goverment**
Maryam Rajavi
July 2017

**Non au Voile Obligatoire
Non à la Religion Obligatoire
Non au Gouvernement Obligatoire**
Maryam Radjavi
July 2017

Great March towards Freedom
Maryam Rajavi
November 2019

**Iran: La grande marche vers
la liberté**
Maryam Rajavi
November 2019

Our Commitments
Maryam Rajavi
July 2020

**Freedom, Democracy and Equality
Maryam Rajavi
July 2021 speeches**